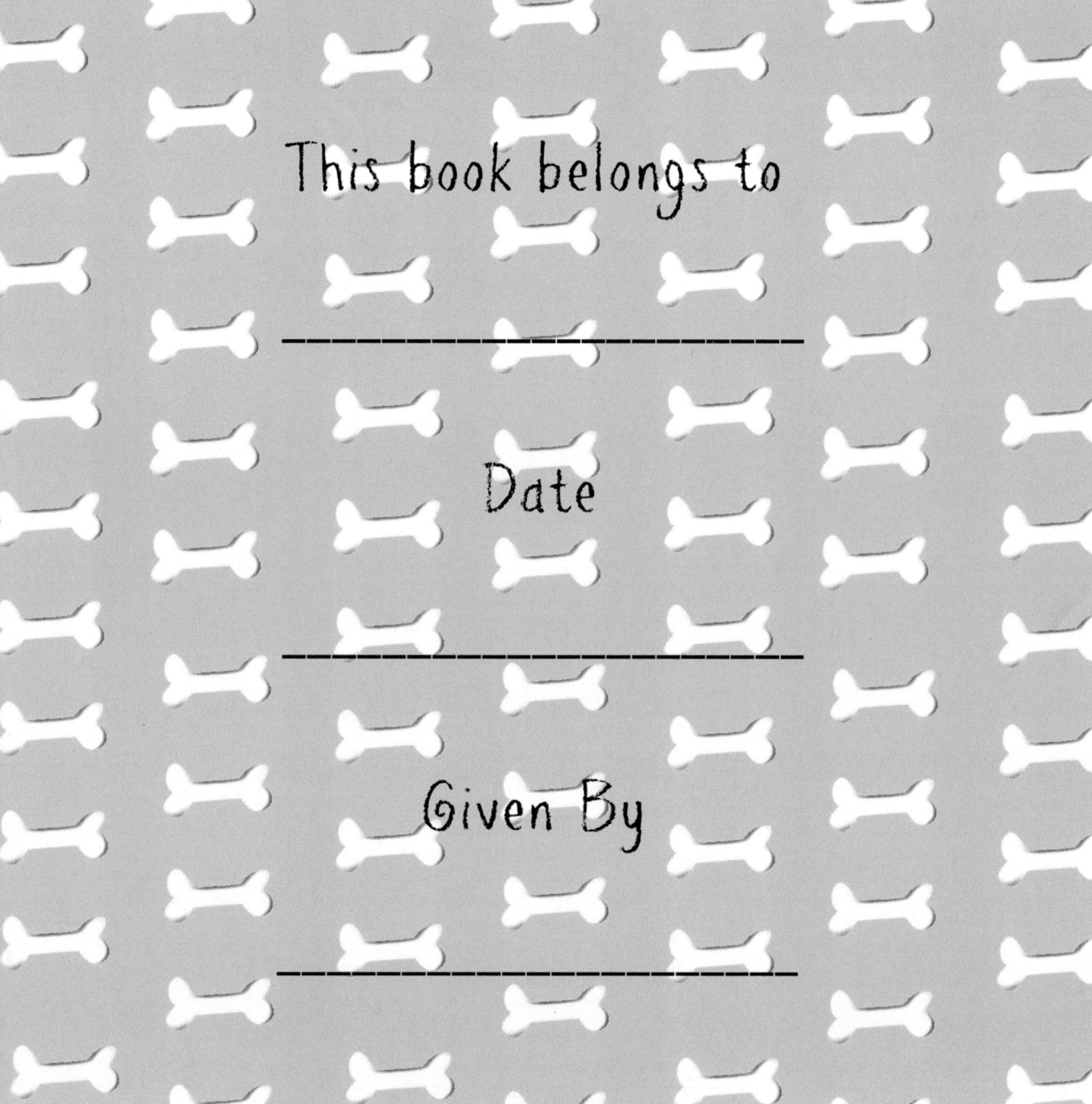

The Littlest Puppy
written by Mary Griffith Chalupsky

All rights reserved
Copyright © 2017
ISBN 13: 978-1547281824
ISBN 10: 1547281820

No part of this book may be copied
transmitted, translated
or reproduced in any manner,
without the written consent from
the author.

Publisher Corridor Pub
Editor: Jim Morrow

mary.chalupsky@yahoo.com

DEDICATION

The Littlest Puppy
"The Littlest Puppy" is dedicated to LaVerne L. Chalupsky,
my husband of 56 years. "The Littlest Puppy" is adapted from a
true story about a little, white, Bichon puppy named Buttons.
Buttons was adopted as a companion for LaVerne at a time when he was
very ill. He would hold his little buddy all the time, and the two became
inseparable. When LaVerne passed away in 2009, Buttons became depressed and
so ill that she wasn't expected to live. The loving, caring and emotional
attachment shown by Buttons for her Daddy seemed almost human.

THE LITTLEST PUPPY

Written by
Mary Griffith Chalupsky

Illustrated by
Sharon Johnson

The littlest puppy tried to open her eyes. She was only two days old and she loved to cuddle. She had two brothers and one sister, so it was crowded where she lived. She would wiggle her nose and smell her bed even though she couldn't see. Her days were spent eating and sleeping. She was the littlest of the four puppies. She was a white ball of fluffy fur.

The puppies grew to be fat and loveable.
When they were old enough to be adopted,
they found homes with
a fireman, a teacher, and a grocer.
The littlest puppy left behind
was lonely. She wanted a family
to love.

The littlest puppy was sad as she lay in the corner of her bed dreaming of the day when a nice family would adopt her. She imagined someone petting her, hugging her, and telling her how wonderful she was. She dreamed of living in a nice, loving home. The littlest puppy fell asleep with those thoughts at night, but she awoke each morning feeling sad that she was still alone.

4.

One day, a nice man and woman came to see the littlest puppy. They held her, petted her, and told her she was special. They wanted to adopt her.
The littlest puppy was given her first bath, and she was truly beautiful.
It was winter and very cold, so the woman placed the littlest puppy inside her coat to keep her warm.
The man and woman took the littlest puppy home with them.

The nice woman and the man adopted the littlest puppy, and they became the littlest puppy's Mama and Daddy. They made a bed for the puppy by placing a soft sweater in a box where the puppy would sleep. They placed a clock next to the puppy. The littlest puppy cuddled beneath the sweater and listened to the clock tick. She fell sound asleep.

Mama and Daddy decided it was time to give the littlest
puppy a name. The names they liked were
Sally, Muffin, Penny and Bailey.
The name had to be just
right for the littlest
ball of fur.

Daddy looked into the littlest
puppy's eyes and whispered,
"You have two black eyes
and a shiny black nose
that looks like a button.
That's it!
We'll call you Buttons!"
Mama also thought Buttons
was a great name for
the littlest puppy.
…So, Buttons became
the littlest puppy's name.

Mama and Daddy bought Buttons a kennel; a safe home where a pet sleeps and hangs out.
All pets should have a safe place where they feel safe and loved. Just like us having our own room for sleep or for watching TV.
A pet likes to go to their safe place when they want to be alone.
They wanted Buttons to feel safe, and she needed enough room to move around with her favorite toy.

Buttons needed a collar and a harness to wear while taking walks with her new family. She needed her own feeding bowl and a bowl to hold her water. Mama bought her a black stuffed dog with a red collar and a red ball with holes for a rope. She loved her new toys. She played with the stuffed dog as if it was a real dog, and she pulled the rope with the ball everywhere. Mama and Daddy laughed at her because she was funny.

Everyday Buttons would do something to make them laugh. When she was awake, Mama or Daddy would take her for a walk. Buttons loved to sleep inside Daddy's vest while he watched television. They would take a nap together, and it became part of their daily routine.

Buttons was happy living with the nice man and the woman. Buttons and her Mama and Daddy cuddled and played together every day.

Daddy had to go on a long trip. Buttons became
sad when she couldn't find her friend.
She ran from room to room, up and down
the steps, looking for Daddy.
When she didn't find him,
she lay down and refused
to eat or drink.
She became sick.
Buttons thought
Daddy was
gone forever. Mama
took Buttons to the
doggy doctor and
the doctor
fed Buttons
through a tube.

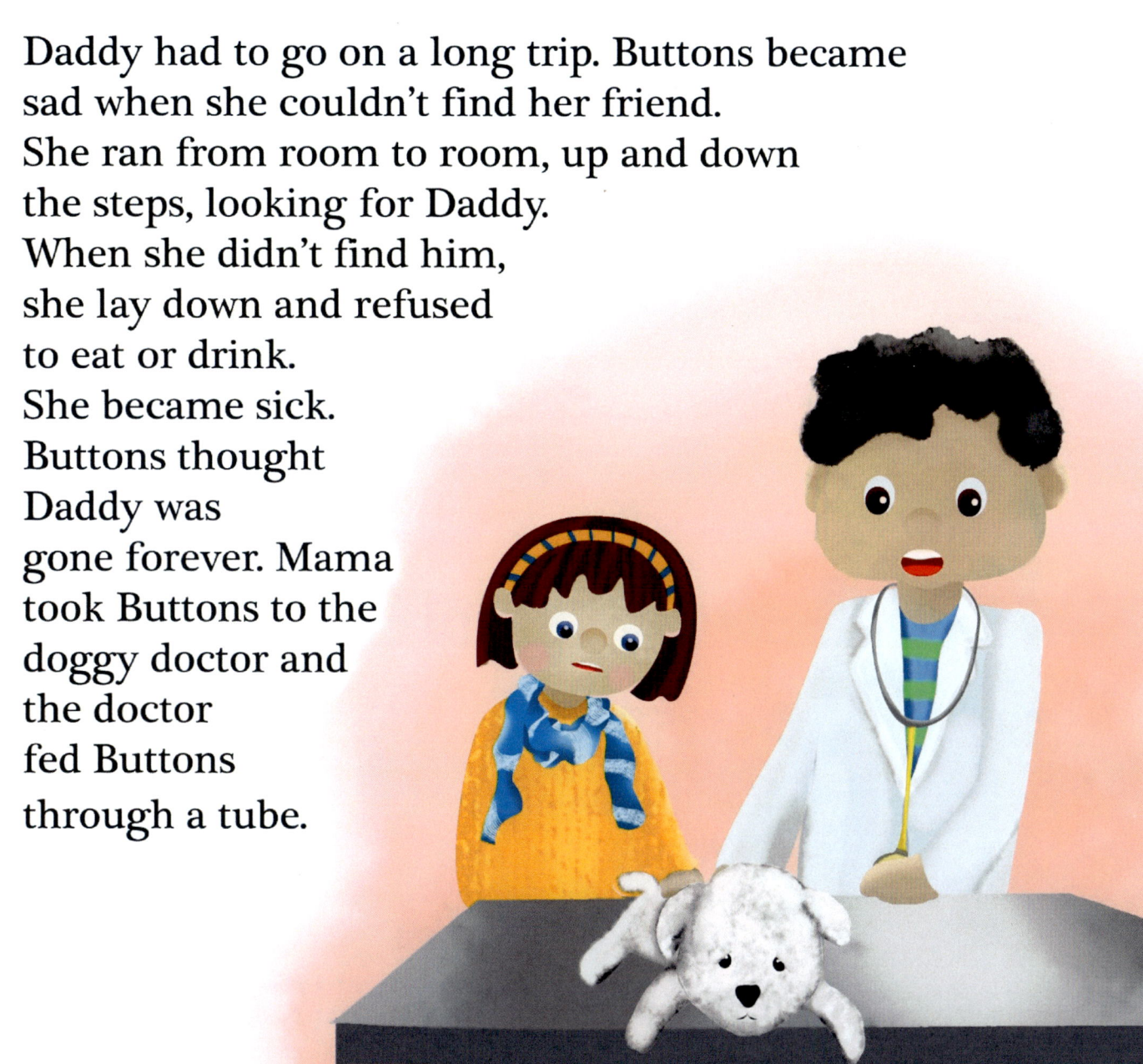

He gave her medicine to make her feel better. Buttons still missed her Daddy and she moped around the house whimpering and whining.
When she couldn't find Daddy she cried herself to sleep every night. Mama tried to soothe her but Buttons was very sad. When Daddy's work was finished, he came home. He received hugs from Mama. Buttons was happy to see Daddy. She licked his face as he patted and hugged her.

Everywhere Daddy went Buttons followed. Daddy took Buttons for her walk each day. He took Buttons to the bank and to the grocery store. Buttons rode with Daddy to the post office and everyone looked forward to seeing Buttons. The lady at the bank always had a treat for Buttons.

Mama brushed Buttons' fur and placed a little pink ribbon in her hair. Daddy bought Buttons a pair of blue sunglasses and placed them on her button nose. They were to protect her eyes from the bright sunlight. Buttons looked like a movie star and everyone loved Buttons.

Buttons was snow white and her fur was beautiful and soft. She loved to jump on Mama's bed and hide in Mama's fluffy, white bedspread.
All that could be seen when she was in the bed, were two black eyes and a black button nose. She looked like a fluffy toy puppy from the toy store until she moved.

Buttons loved to surprise company when they came for a visit. She would hide in the bedspread and it was hard to see her. Then at the last minute she would jump up and surprise them.
The company would laugh because they thought Buttons was special.

Buttons was well-behaved. She learned how to sit and beg. She learned how to roll over, shake hands, and she learned how to fetch a stick.
When company would come, Buttons was so excited to see them she would sit, beg, rollover, shake hands, and fetch, one trick after the other.
She knew she would receive a doggie treat.
Everyone clapped for Buttons.

One spring day when it was raining, Mama let Buttons go outside. When she came inside she had mud on her paws from playing in a mud puddle. Mama was upset. She yelled at Buttons, "You need a bath!" Buttons ran into the bedroom to hide. Taking a bath was one of the things she didn't like.
Mama chased after Buttons. Buttons was tracking mud all over the clean floor.

18.

Without thinking Mama yelled, "Buttons, bathtub!"
Buttons jumped off the bed and ran into another room.
Mama was looking for Buttons and the last place
she looked was the bathroom.
There was Buttons sitting in the bathtub, waiting
for Mama to come give her a bath.

19.

Mama looked at Buttons and laughed,
"Oh Buttons, you are a smarty. You knew what I was telling you, didn't you? I'm proud of you."
From that day on, Buttons was told 'bathtub' once. She would run to the bathroom and jump into the bathtub even though she didn't like her bath.
As long as Mama praised her, Buttons decided a bath wasn't bad after all.

Early one morning the door bell rang. When Mama answered the door there were two little puppies with their Mama Trish. She came to have coffee with Mama and she brought her puppies to play with Buttons. Buttons hid behind her Mama's skirt. She didn't know what a puppy friend was. She was frightened.
"Hi, my name is Salinger," barked the little black puppy with a white beard. "This is my brother, Hayden."

Hayden nodded his head and ran off to the back yard for a stick to share with Buttons. He picked up the stick and dropped it at her feet. Buttons looked at the stick and sniffed.
"Buttons, would you like to play with us?" barked Hayden.
"Why yes, I would," snorted Buttons.
"We can play catch the ball if you like. I'll go get my new ball and we can take turns." "That would be fun," barked Salinger as he ran circles around a tree.

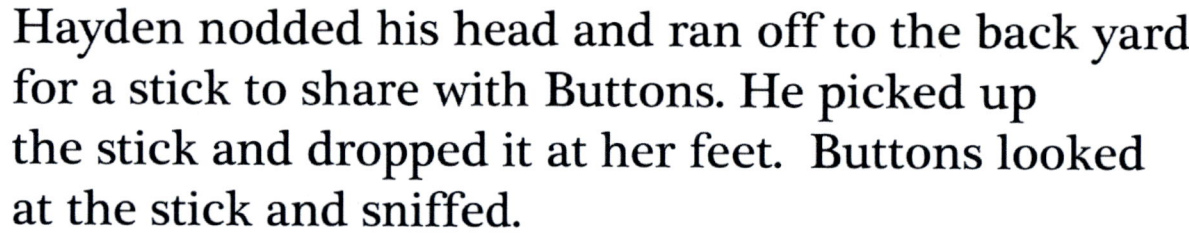

22.

The three puppies played until they were tired. Then they went in the house where Mama served apples, carrots and doggy cookies. They fell sound asleep. When they awoke, they barked their goodbyes and left with their Mama Trish, knowing they would return another day to play with Buttons.

Buttons had a wonderful time with her two new friends. She found her loving family, friends, and her forever home. Mama and Daddy loved her and wanted her as their little puppy. Buttons knew she would never be lonely or sad again.
That evening, Buttons was so happy that she went to sleep with a smile on her face.

Mary Griffith Chalupsky was born Mary Etta Griffith at West Frankfort, IL, to Viola (Brown) and Edgar Griffith.
She was married to LaVerne Chalupsky for 56 years until his death.
Together they raised six children on a farm near Fairfax, Iowa.
She attended Kirkwood College and studied the arts.

Mary began writing poetry many years ago winning awards through the World of Poetry Association, beginning in 1987 when she won the Golden Poet Award and the Award of Merit. The Silver Poet Award followed in 1990 and the Editor Choice Awards in 2005, 2006, and 2007.
She has written and published twelve
Children's Rhyming Picture books called "Jogger's Adventures,"
about a little pig and his animal friends.

She was a volunteer in her church and in her community. She worked in the medical field and owned and operated Medical Claims Billing. Mary served under three state commissions, (Tax Study, Judicial Compensation, and Athletic Trainer) for Iowa Gov. Terry Branstad during his first tenure. She is a member of the DAR and the Mayflower Society.

She worked as a freelancer for Eastern Iowa Online Newspaper, the Arkansas Pacesetting Times, God Makes Lemonade series, and other magazines.

She presently lives in Cedar Rapids, Iowa with her little dog Buttons.

Books By This Author:

How Jogger Got His Name
Jogger Learns to Fish
Jogger Goes to School
Christmas with Jogger
Jogger Goes to the Circus
Jogger's Valentine's
Jogger Drives Big Red
Jogger Goes to the Prom
Jogger Saves the Day
Jogger's New Friends
Jogger Goes to a Car Show
Jogger Goes to the Rodeo
The Littlest Puppy

Made in the USA
Lexington, KY
12 December 2018